THE EUCHARIST
and our everyday life

*

Other books by Bernard Häring CSsR
published by St Paul Publications

Hope is the remedy
Medical Ethics
Faith and morality in a secular age
Sin in the secular age
Evangelization today
Manipulation
Prayer: the integration of faith and life
The sacraments in a secular age
The Beatitudes: their personal and social implications
The Song of the Servant

Bernard Häring CSsR

The
Eucharist

and

our everyday life

St Paul Publications

St Paul Publications
Middlegreen, Slough SL3 6BT

Nihil obstat: D.A. Valente ssp
Imprimatur: F. Diamond vg. Northampton
Copyright: Bernard Haring 1978
First published in Great Britain 1978. Reprinted 1981
Printed by the Society of St Paul. Slough
ISBN 085439 153 3

Contents

Introduction   7
1   Song of praise and mutual blessing   9
2   I shall confess my sins to the praise of
    your mercy   15
3   Every good prayer is praise and thanksgiving   21
4   We hear the word of God and acclaim it   ...   25
5   Alleluia: Praise the Lord   31
6   Messengers of Good News   35
7   Lord, we thank you for the gift of faith   ...   41
8   The Prayer of the Faithful   47
9   Everything is sacred: God's gift   51
10   To render thanks always: the way to salvation   57
11   A grateful memory   63
12   One in Christ, to the glory of God the Father   67
13   In communion with all the Church   71
14   Prayer: joyous, grateful response   75
15   The gift of peace   81
16   Sharers in the divine nature   85
17   Eucharist: gift and mission   91

Introduction

The Second Vatican Council began its great task of reform with the renewal of the liturgy, especially of the Eucharist. Eucharist means *thanksgiving*. And perhaps nothing will be more significant for the new era initiated by Pope John and the Council than the spirit of praise and thanksgiving that celebrates and manifests the Paschal Mystery, the death and resurrection of Christ, his ascension and the effusion of the Holy Spirit.

The decree on the Ministry and Life of Priests (art 5), issued at the conclusion of the Council, re-emphasizes the centrality of the Eucharist for the people of God. "The most blessed Eucharist contains the Church's entire spiritual wealth, that is, Christ himself, our Passover and Bread of Life... Thus the Eucharistic action is the very heartbeat of the congregation of the faithful over which the priest presides. So priests must . . . show the faithful how to sing to the Lord hymns and spiritual songs in their hearts, always giving thanks to God the Father for all things in the name of our Lord, Jesus Christ".

This little book is an act of thanksgiving for the gift of faith and the priestly vocation. It is offered to my fellow priests and the faithful as an invitation to make the Eucharistic thanksgiving and praise the leitmotif and norm for their everyday life, thus bringing home all of their life into the Eucharist.

These meditations are written in hospital after surgery on the vocal chords. When, before the second and most radical intervention, I asked the doctor whether I would ever sing again, he replied kindly, "Even if your voice

may never sing again, your life will praise the Lord".
I was touched that, in so few words, he had got to the
heart of the priestly vocation and, indeed, the vocation
of all Christians.

The whole priestly ministry has as its main purpose
"the adoration of God, our Father, in spirit and truth".
Therefore, the priest should be a leader in the praise of
God; but equally he has to be a learner.

I would be most happy if, in the following pages,
priests and lay people would meditate with me in a
shared desire to learn and to implore together the
greatest art of our life: to adore and praise God with
all our being, to turn together to Christ in the Eucharist
and let him be our teacher, asking nothing more insistently than this: "Lord, teach us to pray, and how to
unite ourselves with you in praise of the Father, by the
gift of the Spirit".

1

Song of praise and mutual blessing

"Let the Holy Spirit fill you; speak to one another in psalms, hymns and songs; sing and make music in your hearts to the Lord; and in the name of our Lord Jesus Christ, give thanks every day for everything to our God and Father" (Eph 5:18-20).

Normally, the Eucharist begins and ends with a song of praise and joy. We should bring home all our joys into the liturgy. We have listened to heaven and earth as they "proclaim the glory of God". We have been warmed by the sun and have heard the music of the earth. We have admired the beauty of flowers. The smiles of children, reflecting the love of their parents, brothers, sisters and friends, have delighted us. And the signs of goodness, gentleness, generosity that we have seen and received are countless.

All this comes to full life and truth when we bring it before the Lord in a song of gratitude and joy. So why should not our joy grow in depth and breadth when our own voices are joined with others in one melody in praise of God? How marvellous a gift is our voice: to communicate with each other, to express our feelings, our heart, and to bring forth melodies that resound all over the world!

But perhaps you, my friend, may tell me: "I am saddened by so many things, there is so much suffering in my life and around me, how can I sing songs of praise and joy?"

Only the Eucharist, in its deepest meaning, can give you the answer. We are redeemed; our sorrows, too, can praise the Lord who has borne our sufferings and has thus given to suffering a new meaning. If we truly enter into the Eucharist, all this can be understood as a blessing, as a means of purification, as a humble yet important share in the redemption of the world.

In the light of the Paschal Mystery which we celebrate, there is nothing that could prevent us from singing songs of praise and thus blessing each other. St Paul sends his most touching blessings and hymns of thanksgiving from prison. There, too, and especially there, he proclaims the Good News. And there he comes closer to Christ. "My only desire is to know Christ, to experience the power of his resurrection. I want to suffer and to die in union with him, so that I, too, shall arrive at the resurrection from the dead" (Phil 3:10-11). So he can exhort his fellow Christians, "Rejoice in the Lord. I repeat it, rejoice always" (Phil 4:4).

St Francis of Assisi composed his marvellous song of praise, inviting brother Sun and sister Moon and all creatures to join him, when he was gravely ill and about to lose the sight of his eyes. He completed it in the hour when the Lord called him by his beloved sister Death.

This is the sign of redemption of everything, even of death — above all, of death. Everything can and will bring us closer to the Lord and the power of his resurrection if we live the morality of the Paschal Mystery in praise and gratitude.

Anyone who is transformed by this mystery of Eucharist, of praise and thanksgiving, becomes a blessing for his fellow travellers. It is not surprising that Saint Francis instinctively recognized this connection. For himself and his disciples he made it a rule to greet everyone with the biblical blessing, "Peace be with you"; "Pax et Bene".

If we have a fine ear for the cosmic liturgy of praise,

and bring it home into the Eucharist, we realize ever better how we become mutual sources of blessing for each other. Everyone we meet, and especially those with whom we join hands in life, becomes for us a motive for praising God for, as Eucharistic people, we first discover in everyone the good that comes from God and helps us on the road to God. It is in this reciprocal appreciation and in this shared praise of God that we become a real blessing for each other.

The first event in the Eucharistic celebration, after the song of joy, is the exchange of blessings between the priest and the other participants. The Mass begins and ends with a blessing, for we are meant to be and to become ever more, in Christ, a mutual source of joy, of peace, of goodness, of gentleness and of every other blessing. Whenever we meet each other there is a time of favour to radiate and to rejoice in peace and goodness, to make known the marvellous deeds of God and to ask God's blessing on each other.

To bless everyone and everything, to bring to all people the joy and peace of the Lord, is among the principal functions of the priest, but not of him alone. He fulfils his mission to the extent that all the faithful come to realize that this is their privilege, too.

The priest greets and blesses with the words, "The Lord be with you", and the participants reply with the meaningful words, "and with your spirit" or "and also with you". The Lord is always with us with his creative power; but what we implore in our blessing is that we may become fully aware of his loving presence and ever more responsive. Then our spirit will rejoice in God our Saviour, as Mary sings in the song of her life.

When a bishop is the celebrant, his usual greeting is "Peace be with you". His role, among other things, is to be, above all, a peacemaker and to invite all Christians to join Christ, the Prince of Peace, and to

11

rejoice that, as children of God, they are called to act as peaceful and peace-bringing people.

St Paul begins almost all his letters with the prayer of blessing: "Grace and peace from God our Father and from our Lord Jesus Christ". This includes, indeed, all that is good. It is also an invitation to turn our grateful attention to these wonderful, undeserved gifts of God, and thus become fully receptive to them.

"Grace" is God's own graciousness, his fatherly love. Christ has come to make this graciousness fully visible to us. If we open ourselves to the grace and peace that come to us from the Father through Christ, we too become gracious, gentle, a kind of sacramental sign of God's own graciousness. Thus we are, in Christ, a source of blessing for each other.

Frequently we use at the beginning of the Mass the blessing with which St Paul concludes his second letter to the Corinthians: "The grace of our Lord Jesus Christ, the love of God our Father, and the fellowship of the Holy Spirit be with you all". And again the people return this greeting and blessing in the mutuality of brothers and sisters. What a joy it is for the priest to be able to bless and to receive back the blessing multiplied by the participants! This forms a profound bond of mutual gratitude, reverence, trust and solidarity. Our full awareness of this dimension is important for the Eucharistic community and for all our relationships as they flow from the Eucharist and return to it.

When I came home as a newly ordained priest after six years of complete absence, the first thing I did was to give my parents, brothers and sisters the priest's blessing. Late that evening, when it was about time to retire, my mother asked gently, "May I still give you my blessing as I always did in the past?" My response was, "By all means! If I can now bless people, was not your blessing and father's the beginning of all this?"

Our mutual blessing in the Eucharist and the family blessing in the evening should be an abiding presence. It should mould a consciousness and openness that can transform our whole life, bringing us closer to each other and helping each other to come closer to God in gratitude and trust.

In old Christian cultures it was and is still a good practice to bless each other with the praise of God on meeting and parting: "Praised be Jesus Christ" — "now and forever"; "God keep and protect you" — "and you too"; "Go with God" — "Stay with God", and similar forms. We need people like Francis to reintroduce, courageously and graciously, appropriate expressions of the reciprocal blessing and shared praise of God.

God, our Father,
we praise you for the many signs of your love.
Let your countenance shine upon us all,
so that we remind each other of your gracious presence
and together praise your name.

Jesus Christ, our Lord and brother,
manifest to all the attractive power of your grace.
Draw us all together in your kindness,
making us a sign of unity
and thus a blessing for all of mankind.
On your cross you have prayed for all,
even for those
who drove the nails into your hands and feet.
You are a blessing
not only for your beloved mother and the faithful disciple
but for all.
By your example you teach us to bless
even those who curse us.
Make us a source of grace and blessing
for all people,
especially for those who hurt us.

13

Come, Holy Spirit, Spirit of Truth,
Make us holy, make us one in your truth.
Fill our hearts with your joy,
so that we may gratefully sing
the praise of the Father, through Jesus Christ,
with one heart and in one spirit.
Amen.

2

I shall confess my sins to the praise of your mercy

"So I advised you to buy from me gold refined in the fire, to make you truly rich, and white clothes to put on to hide the shame of your nakedness, and ointment for your eyes so that you may see. All whom I love I reproach and discipline. Be on your mettle therefore, and repent. Here I stand knocking at the door; if anyone hears my voice and opens the door, I will come in and sit down to supper with him and he with me" (Rev 3:18-21).

In the earliest days of the Church, the spontaneous confession before the priest, and especially the penitential rite with the general confession at the beginning of the Mass, was called *confessio laudis*, meaning confession for our sins to the praise of God's mercy.

It is essential to see each part of the Eucharist in the whole picture. Each part increases the beauty of the whole. Penance, too, is Eucharist; that is, thanksgiving. We shall never understand the profound meaning of the Eucharistic sacrifice without great gratitude for the remission of our sins. The blood of the Redeemer is shed for us "so that sins may be forgiven".

Understood as confession of sins to the praise of God's goodness, the penitential rite is not something apart. Rather, it opens and introduces a dimension that pervades the whole celebration from beginning to end and illumines a fundamental aspect of our whole life. The memorial of the Lord's death and resurrection brings forth in us a wonderful contrast-harmony of holy fear in view of God's holiness and exultant joy because of his fatherly goodness.

We honour God and come closer to salvation if the sorrow for our sins is expressed with great *trust* in God's compassionate love. This trust becomes abiding gratitude and praise. Indeed, our sorrow is proved authentic only through trust and gratitude; and it is these attitudes which then bring an important change in all our relationships: with God, with self and with all whom we meet. We come to know God no longer as a threat but as the giver of all good gifts, as the Healer. Thus we can pray, "Heal me, Lord, for I have sinned". Even if the deep experience of our sinfulness might tempt us to say, "Lord, go away from me; I am a sinner", the revelation of his healing compassion makes us pray, "Where should we go? You alone have words of salvation".

It is in our deep gratitude for God's healing mercy that we feel at home with him. We are accepted; we can therefore accept ourselves, our shades, and our need of further conversion and purification. And we praise the Lord for all the opportunities (frustrations, sufferings, tensions) that he sends us in order to complete his work in us.

From this same gratitude arises our capacity to open ourselves to our fellow travellers with their shades, faults and needs of further conversion. If the confession of our sins is truly permeated by praise and thanksgiving, then it will be natural for us to forgive, spontaneously and wholeheartedly, those who offend us. How small are these offences against our inflated majesty if we compare them with our own offences against the all-holy God! Pope John XXIII had a deep understanding of this dimension. Early in his life, he wrote in his spiritual diary: "After each sin I shall, as soon as possible, make an act of sorrow and of great, great trust. And then I shall say to myself, 'John, go ahead as if Jesus had given you a kiss' ".

A better understanding of the penitential rite within the total beauty of the Eucharist gives us also a new access to the sacrament of reconciliation. We shall rejoice that, through God's grace, we are able to confess our sins with trust, and open ourselves ever more to the messianic peace. And we shall never dissociate the sacramental reparation from thanksgiving. For we shall then ask not so much. "What punishment have I deserved for so many sins?" but rather, "How can I now show my gratitude for God's great kindness and healing forgiveness?".

Not seldom have I given to penitents who came from a great spiritual distance and had a long way to go, instead of a formal penance, the task of examining themselves daily for a certain period on "How did I thank the Lord today for his generosity, kindness, forgiveness, and how shall I thank him still better tomorrow?" The results have sometimes been astonishing. Yet, many who scrupulously confess their sins are not really converted because they offer no actual penance-reparation; and this is so because of lack of gratitude.

Some people refuse the confession of their sins because they have no insight into this Eucharistic dimension. They fail to realize that God's healing forgiveness is undeserved, an absolutely gratuitous gift. Yet, this very gratuitousness tells us that we do not open ourselves to the gift unless we acknowledge this gratuity through a humble and grateful confession.

If we understand and practice all this, our everyday life will change substantially. We shall be grateful to our neighbour who accepts us as we are and forgives us generously. We shall have the courage to acknowl-

17

edge our faults and ask for forgiveness and, of course, we shall forgive from the bottom of our hearts those who have grieved us.

I know some very fine Christian families who, each evening, celebrate a kind of "confessio laudis". They examine together the events of the day in order to see all the good, to acknowledge humbly the shortcomings, and to assure each other full forgiveness; then they praise God together for acting patiently with them. This is both a good preparation for the Eucharistic celebration and the sacrament of reconciliation, and a beautiful harvest of liturgical spirituality. It transforms the whole family life.

In past theology there were many disputes about the difference between imperfect sorrow (attrition) and contrition. I think that full attention to the dimension of praise and thanksgiving is the very best help and criterion for assuring a truly saving contrition.

God, our Father,
it is hard to confess faults before a severe judge,
but it is something quite different
to open our hearts and to confess our sins before you.
For, in Jesus Christ,
you have revealed your great compassion
and the healing power of your love.
Grant that our confession and sorrow
may always give praise to your name as Father,
and to the name of Jesus,
the Good Shepherd, the Divine Healer,
the Prince of Peace,
who is the perfect sacrament of your mercy and kindness.
Let your Holy Spirit mould our hearts
so that our confession of sins becomes truly
a Eucharistic praise of your mercy.
Grant that our willingness
to acknowledge humbly our faults before our neighbour,
and readily forgive his faults,

may continue the Eucharistic praise
and prepare us to participate in it more fully.

Lord, I want to thank you now, especially
because in my past life there was a lack of gratitude.
I pray that others, too, may come to understand better
the wonderful privilege of thanking you and praising you,
particularly in view of the forgiveness of our past sins.

May each Eucharistic celebration
increase our gratitude and praise for your healing love.
Amen.

3

Every good prayer is praise and thanksgiving

"The Lord is near; have no anxiety, but in every-thing make your requests known to God in prayer and petition with thanksgiving. Then the peace of God, which is beyond understanding, will keep guard over your hearts and your thoughts, in Christ Jesus" (Phil 4:6-7).

The "Collect", the special prayer of the Church, is preceded on Sundays and Feastdays by the "Gloria". This prayer is a most beautiful synthesis of praise and humble petition.

Surely the praise could not be offered more heartily if we were to forget our own needs. The Christmas message has already shown us that God's glory and our own salvation cannot be severed. God magnifies his name of "Father" by his concern for our salvation. In response, we open ourselves to God's grace and attain our salvation by our desire to adore him and to render thanks always. Only through the synthesis of prayer of petition and prayer of thanksgiving do we come to acknowledge, truly and fully, that "You alone are the Lord; you alone are the Most High . . .".

Forty years ago, at the passionate beginning of the liturgical renewal, we frequently disputed whether prayer of praise or prayer of petition is more fitting and central to the liturgy and in our personal relationship with God. St Paul gives us the true solution. He constantly renders thanks but also offers petitions and supplications. Repeatedly, he shows the real synthesis by exhorting the communities to offer prayer *with thanksgiving*.

Through humble and persevering petition we gratefully acknowledge our total dependence on God. We praise the gratuity of his gifts, especially the grace of perseverance. Our thanksgiving would be lacking if our constant awareness of how much we are in need of God were not expressed. Indeed, the humble prayer of petition is an essential part of the first beatitude: "How blessed are those who know their need of God" (Mt 5:3); and it must be filled with gratitude, for we shall never be able to count all the reasons we have for thanking God for his gifts and his goodness.

Our very dependence on God is enough reason for joy, praise and thanksgiving, for God has revealed himself as our almighty Father. To pray to him means to rest in him, to be confidently at home with him who is the source and final goal of our existence. There we come to an ever deeper understanding of the truth of being and of the uniqueness of our name by which God calls us, and calls us to be with him.

A special reason for joyful prayer is the honour of praying in the name of Jesus. If we put our trust in him, then we know that the Father loves us as he loves Jesus, and accepts our prayers as if they came from him. When we pray in the name of Jesus, we are not alone; we are led by the Spirit who makes us cry out with Jesus, "*Abba*, Father!"

And being united with Jesus means to be in and to pray in the communion of saints: with Mary our Mother and with all the elect in heaven and on earth. During his imprisonment, the Protestant theologian and martyr Dietrich Bonhoeffer found special consolation in the experience of intercession. He felt the support of the prayers of all his friends, and it was equally comforting for him to offer his intercession for all. Prayer is frequently a mysterious communication in the communion of saints. It is, especially in the liturgy, a grateful and responsive experience of our solidarity of salvation before the one God and Father, through the one Saviour and Mediator, Jesus Christ, in the one Spirit.

We pray thankfully because we know that God listens to us. He knows our needs even before we spell them out. Before him, in trustful prayer, we come to a better self-understanding. Everything enters into a proper perspective. While we express our desires, we already thank God for whatever response he decides to give us, because we know that it will be given by him who is Love.

Our prayer is, above all, for the conformity of our will with the loving will of the Father, for growth in faith, growth in the knowledge of his holy name, in wisdom, peace and generosity. "And this is my prayer, that your love may grow ever richer and richer in knowledge and insight of every kind, and may thus bring you the gift of true discrimination. Then on the Day of Christ you will be flawless and without blame, reaping the full harvest of righteousness that comes through Jesus Christ, to the glory and praise of God" (Phil 1: 9-11).

Quite as much as in the prayer of praise and thanksgiving, in the proper prayer of petition God is, and becomes ever more effectively, the centre of our life. We pray that all our being, our desires, words and deeds may be consistent with our faith, and thus honour God.

If our prayers are not inspired, filled and followed by thanksgiving, then we should realize that we have not yet really found the Eucharistic dimension: God is not yet fully at the centre of our life. How insensitive are the prayers of those who show no interest in celebrating the Eucharist with God's people, who do not feel any inner need to render thanks with the whole

23

Church, but pray only when they want something from God! Yet, to cry to God in one's distress can become a conversion when those cries open the horizon of trust and gratitude.

Many God-fearing people of various religions feel so strongly that prayers without gratitude have no value, that they bind themselves by vow to offer signs of gratitude. The Psalmist expresses this attitude beautifully: "What can I render to the Lord for whatever he has given me? I shall take the chalice of salvation and call upon the name of the Lord. I shall fulfil my vows to the Lord in the sight of all his people" (Ps 116:12-14).

We thank you, Father, Lord of heaven and earth,
for having revealed to us,
through your beloved Son Jesus Christ,
that you are always present to us with all your love
ready to hear our prayers.
What a joy to know
that we can always entrust ourselves to you!
May your Holy Spirit come upon us and cleanse us,
so that we may ever more gratefully experience
the privilege of praying with filial confidence.
Send us your light, that we may always pray
for those things that honour your name.
And give us the grace to be especially grateful
for those gifts that puzzle us
or take us by surprise.
We ask this through Christ our Lord.
Amen.

4

We hear the word of God
and acclaim it

"For just as the rain and snow come down from
the heavens and do not return there till they have
watered the earth, making it fertile and fruitful,
giving seed to him who sows and bread to him
who eats, so shall my word be that goes forth
from my mouth; it shall not return to me void,
but shall do my will, achieving the end for which
I sent it" (Is 55:10-11).

It is one thing to study the Bible as a literary document but quite another thing to meditate on it in
profound awareness of the presence of the One whose
word speaks to us.

The Eucharistic celebration is the most appropriate
occasion for hearing the word of God and rejoicing in
it, for there we meet Christ, the Word Incarnate, in the
celebration of a community of grateful believers.

Wherever we have had the privilege of celebrating in
a joyous, grateful community, we have been touched by
the warmth of the response, "Thanks be to God",
"Praise to you, Lord Jesus Christ". Whether we
expressed our thanks in explicit words or not, we realized
that where there is no spirit of thankfulness and praise,
this priceless gift, the Word of God is practically refused
and lost.

Grateful listening to the Word of God is a fundamental part of prayer, and especially of the Eucharist. When we truly open ourselves to Christ, the living and life-giving Word of the Father, then we will respond to him with heart and mind, with our will and the best of our passions, in prayer and in the whole of our lives.

Let us, time and again, recall the many reasons for gratitude that, in the celebration of the Eucharist and on other occasions in a vital community of faith, we can receive the Good News coming from God and reaching into the depth of our being. The Second Vatican Council gives us this profound reason: "Christ is present in his word, since it is he himself who speaks when the holy Scriptures are read in the Church. He is present, finally, when the Church prays and sings, for he promised that 'Where two or three are gathered for my sake, there am I in the midst of them' (Mt 18:20)" (Constitution on the Sacred Liturgy, 7).

True, Christ's Eucharistic presence as such, is Good News in the deepest sense: "I died for you, I am risen for you, I live for you, I want to live in you". But only those who listen attentively to Holy Scripture will be fully touched by this Good News.

Christ himself is the Good News coming from the Father. For those who are open to his Spirit, his words are "spirit and life" (Jn 6:63). Through his word, and through the mission of the Holy Spirit, he gathers his Church and makes her his body, nourished by his body and his word. The Catechism of the Council of Trent sees the Church as "the rallying call" (convocation) wherein Christ calls us to unity and solidarity.

We cannot, therefore, worthily thank Christ, the Word Incarnate, who unites us in the love of the Father, by the power of the Holy Spirit, without simultaneously feeling profound gratitude also for the Church, the community of faith. For through her, Christ shares with us the Good News and helps us to rejoice in his word, to celebrate it and to understand its challenge for our life.

Those who receive the word of God in the Eucharist with heartfelt gratitude will gradually acquire a *grateful memory*. They will take time to read and to meditate on the holy Scriptures, and will treasure the memory of all that God has done for us.

In the inspiring little book *The Hiding Place*, we meet the two brave sisters, Corrie and Betsie ten Boom, who were seized by the Nazis for hiding Jews in their home in Holland. When they were finally brought to the camp of destruction and pushed into a filthy barrack overcrowded with despairing prisoners, they had saved nothing except a little Bible hidden under their poor clothes. Corrie praised the Lord for this great treasure, and Betsie continued the litany of thanksgiving: "Praise the Lord, for he sends us to minister his word here, where there is such great need". And then, day by day, they shared this treasure, the word of God, with their fellow prisoners, and created a new spirit. The deadened souls of the prisoners came alive again. They overcame hatred, even to the point that one of the most terrifying supervisors was changed and learned compassion. Such is the power of the gratefully shared meditation on the word of God.

In the Eucharistic discourse (Jn 6) Jesus presents himself as the life-giving bread. He shares himself in a way symbolized by the bread that gives itself up to nourish people. Jesus himself lives by his unique union with the Eternal Word that comes from the Father. He is total, grateful attention to the Father's word and will. And sharing the Good News and his very self with us, he admonishes us that "Man does not live by bread alone, but by every word that comes from God" (Mt 4:4).

There is a sublime synthesis in the discourse, between the way Jesus nourishes and transforms us by his word, the Good News, and by his Eucharistic body and blood.

The more eagerly we receive his word, the more we will experience the new life that comes to us through his body and his blood. To the extent that the word of God takes root in us, we shall rejoice in our union with him in the Eucharist. "Abide in me, and I shall dwell in you . . . I am the vine, you are the branches . . . If you abide in me and my words take root in you, ask for whatever you want, ask what you will, it will be done for you. My Father has been glorified by your bearing much fruit and becoming my disciples" (Jn 15:4-8).

Often we come to the Eucharist or to the meditation of the word of God under the burden of suffering and sin. The Good News sheds its light on our suffering and shakes us at the thought of our sins. It calls us to that sorrow that prepares our hearts for consolation and re-newed joy.

This point is brought home movingly in the book of Nehemiah. The people were in great distress when they had returned from exile. They met not only wild beasts but also the enmity of the inhabitants of the land. The governor Nehemiah and the priest Esdras gathered them to hear the Scriptures. The words were read clearly and explained, and their hearts were touched. All wept. The priest Esdras told them, "This day is holy to the Lord your God. Do not be sad, do not weep . . . Go, prepare a feast, and allot a portion to those who have nothing ready . . . Do not be saddened this day, for rejoicing in the Lord must be your strength" (Neh 8:9-10).

Our first response to the Good News is not a con-crete purpose to *do* something, but is joy, purifying sorrow, trust, gratitude. From this the good resolutions are born, and the strength to put them into practice. The word of God is always first a gift and then — and thus — a call, a challenge, and the strength for com-mitment. It reaches us in a concrete historical moment and illumines our way.

28

Moreover, when we celebrate and meditate together on the word of God, this helps us to decipher the "signs of the times", to discover the opportunities given us to do good and to withstand what is evil, to respond to the most crying needs of our neighbours and of the community and society. "The light transforms whatever it illumines, and all that appears is light. That is why we read, 'Sleeper, awake, arise from the dead, and Christ will give you light'. Keep careful watch over your conduct. Do not act like fools but like thoughtful men. Make the most of the present opportunity" (Eph 5:14-16).

By continually meditating on the word of God in a spirit of gratitude, we gain a great vision of the history of salvation and see all events in a new light and perspective. And our response will always be, "Lord, here I am, call me; send me".

Lord, grant us a grateful heart and memory
so that your word can take root in us.
Let us rejoice in your presence and in your Gospel,
so that each of us and our whole community
may become a living Gospel
for our neighbour and for all to whom we reach out.
Let us never cease to praise you for your life-giving word.
Amen.

5

Alleluia: Praise the Lord

"After this I heard what sounded like the loud song of a great assembly in heaven. They were singing: 'Alleluia! Salvation, glory and might belong to our God, for his judgments are true and just! He has condemned the great harlot who corrupted the earth with her harlotry. He has avenged the blood of his servants which was shed by her hand.

"Once more they sang 'Alleluia!' And as the smoke began to rise from her forever and ever, the four and twenty elders and the four living creatures fell down and worshipped God seated on the throne and sang, 'Amen! Alleluia!'

"A voice coming from the throne cried out: 'Praise our God, all you servants, the small and the great, who revere him!' Then I heard what sounded like the shouts of a great crowd or the roaring of the deep, or mighty peals of thunder, as they cried: 'Alleluia! The Lord is king, our God, the Almighty! Let us rejoice and be glad, and give him glory! For this is the wedding day of the Lamb; his bride has prepared herself for the wedding'" (Rev 19:1-8).

This triumphant song of praise from the Apocalypse makes us aware that our celebrations, our joys and sorrows, our shared witness and actions, are already united with the heavenly Jerusalem if, in our own life, everything is accepted, done and offered to the praise of God. Many of our friends, members of our family and community have already made their passage to the everlasting 'Alleluia'. We rejoice with them and thank them by our songs of joy.

Gratitude for the word of God, for the experience of the solidarity of salvation, for our union in Christ, shows us the way. Our 'Alleluia' does not at all take us away from the earthly task but rather gives us clear direction, sober motives and abiding strength.

B.F. Skinner and his whole school of behaviourism present us with the sad picture of ourselves as a species completely conditioned by our environment and shaped by the twin masters of pain and pleasure. Down payment in remuneration for instant happiness and fear of punishment are the only motives they recognise. They promise survival of the human race or of one's own group only to those who give up the idea of freedom and dignity and allow the behaviour technologist to manipulate them thoroughly and scientifically. The utilitarian outlook allows the mind-managers to perfect the tactics and manoeuvres of brain washing.

The sad truth is that the behaviourists are right insofar as those people are concerned who live on the merely contractual, commercial level of motives: "You give me and I will give you". Parents, who are unable or unwilling to give their children selfless love and give them instead a lot of things in order to alleviate the caretaker's troubles, play into the hands of these behaviourists.

But, thanks be to God, the skillful manipulators will have no power over those whose life is an 'Alleluia': people who are motivated by joy, praise, thanksgiving, grateful appreciation for all that is good, and wonder for all that is beautiful, the splendour of truth and goodness. They are not marked by the sign of the beast that rises from the abyss. They will bring forth fruit in love, peace, generosity, gentleness, non-violent commitment to justice and freedom. They will respect and promote everyone's dignity.

Our earth loses everything, even the hope of survival, if people consider the praise of God and songs of thanksgiving and joy as waste of time and energy. The joyous celebrations of faith that respond to God's gratuitous love have their worth in themselves. They express the truth of our being; and by that very fact they are, at the same time, an immense blessing for us and for all whom we meet.

We speak here of the Alleluias not only as a part of the Eucharist: the part is, rather, in the whole, and the whole is present in the part. The Eucharist, the centre of our Christian life, is praise, thanksgiving, rejoicing. If the celebration is genuine, all our life will sing the praise of God.

"Praise the Lord for he is good; sing praise to our God, for he is gracious; it is fitting to praise him. The Lord rebuilds Jerusalem; the dispersed of Israel he gathers. He heals the broken-hearted and binds up their wounds. He tells the number of the stars; he calls each by name. Great is our Lord and mighty in power; to his wisdom there is no limit. The Lord sustains the lowly; the wicked he casts to the ground.

"Sing to the Lord with thanksgiving; sing praise with the harp to our God. Who covers the heavens with clouds, who provides rain for the earth; who makes grass sprout on the mountains, and herbs for the service of men; who gives food to the cattle and to the young ravens when they cry to him. In the strength of the steed he delights not, nor is he pleased with the fleetness of men. The Lord is pleased with those who fear him, with those who hope for his kindness.

"Glorify the Lord, O Jerusalem; praise your God, O Zion! For he has strengthened the bars of your gates; he has blessed your children within you. He has granted peace in your borders; with the best of wheat

33

C

he fills you. He sends forth his command to the earth; swiftly runs his word! He spreads snow like wool; frost he strews like ashes. He scatters his hail like crumbs; before his cold the waters freeze. He sends his word and melts them; he lets his breeze blow and the waters run. He has proclaimed his word to Jacob, his statutes and his ordinances to Israel. He has not done this for any other nation; his ordinances he has not made known to them. Alleluia!" (Ps 147).

God, our Father,
you have created everything to the praise of your glory.
And you glorify your name through your gifts to us.
We can share in your goodness, truth and beauty
by praising your name.
We thank you for having sent us your Son, Jesus Christ,
to give you praise also in our name,
even on the cross and through his death.
    We thank you, Lord Jesus Christ,
for the gift of the Eucharist,
where you yourself lead us
in the praise of the Father,
in the joy of the Spirit.
    Lord, we pray for priests
and all your priestly people,
that they may realize ever more
the great privilege of songs of joy,
of the celebration of your great glory,
of life that can be fully "Eucharist" with you,
an everlasting, all-embracing 'Alleluia'.
Help us to celebrate worthily and rejoice before you,
so that all our life receives
light and clear direction:
the purpose you have set before us.
Amen.

6

Messengers of Good News

"Very early next morning he got up and went out. He went away to a lonely spot and remained there in prayer. But Simon and his companions searched him out, found him and said, 'They are all looking for you'. He answered, 'Let us move on to the country towns in the neighbourhood; I have to proclaim my message there also; that is what I came out to do'" (Mk 1:35-38).

Jesus, whom his disciples find at prayer, tells us this life-giving truth: that he has come from the Father for this purpose, to share everywhere and with all people his joyous message, the Good News. He is the Master and model not only of the priest but of the whole priestly people of God.

It is our great privilege to join Jesus and to carry out the gracious command which he has given the Church as its main purpose: to pray and proclaim the Good News. And he has assured her of his own gracious presence and of his Spirit wherever and whenever she faithfully discharges this mission. The Eucharist is the summit of all this. The future of the Church and of the evangelization of humankind will greatly depend on how the Christian communities celebrate the memorial of the Lord's death and resurrection.

Here we treat of the homily, but again in a holistic vision. In the homily there must be a full awareness of the whole Eucharist, since only the whole is the complete proclamation of the Good News. But it is not the priest or deacon alone who acts as herald of the Good News. As celebrant and homilist I have frequently experienced how the community has lifted me up and inspired me. Indeed, I have received the Gospel as much from lay people — my parents and many others — as from priests. If the priest lives in a divine milieu of faith and joy, his homily, his whole celebration, life and activity will reflect it, and the laity will surely more than re-echo the words of the priest.

When I was a boy, my father used to gather us at home after the Sunday Mass, sometimes even in the presence of visiting friends or neighbours. He asked each of us what message we had received from the pastor's homily. Then, at the end, he would share with us what he had especially noted. I remember that the simple, direct words of my father impressed me more than the long sermon of the pastor.

The Second Vatican Council has this to say: "Christians spouses are cooperators in grace and witnesses of faith for each other, their children and all others in their household. They are the first to share the faith joyously with their children and to educate them. By word and witness they prepare their offspring for the Christian and apostolic life" (Decree on the Apostolate of the Laity, 11).

The loftiness of the priest's task as preacher of the Good News does not reduce the laity to second-class citizens. The purpose is always that all lay people as well as priests should become true adorers of God, each a living Gospel for the world. The "Amen" after the prayers and homily is not all that we expect from the faithful. Amen ("thus be it in truth") is a weighty word that calls for a whole life of cooperation and witness.

The liturgical renewal has very much emphasized the active role of all participants in the Eucharist. From there will come a more active participation of all believers in the evangelization of the world. This "evangelization" is not at all just the teaching of doctrine, but, even more, a sharing of the joy and beauty of our faith and hope, a reflection of the love of God which we experience.

In organized communities and groups, the shared homily is a very good step. This is not, however, the most decisive initiative, and surely not the first. There are many other opportunities for dialogue of faith. Charismatic and other prayer groups already do much; and I know by experience that priests have profited greatly by all this. Some remark on how their own homilies have benefited from it. I like also the idea of preparing the homily and, indeed, the whole celebration, with a group of religious and lay people.

This common task is particularly evident in the Eucharistic education of children. Children are, by nature, hero worshippers; if everything is normal, their parents, above all, are their heroes. If the Eucharistic message comes first and foremost in the classroom, from a priest or nun, this may still be a beautiful experience but it is quite different if it comes from the parents, and in connection with the basic experiences of home life such as the family meal. Then it is real life, provided, however, that the parents can share a joyous and grateful faith. The priest's task is to help parents understand their own beautiful mission.

If we live with Christ and desire above all else to progress in the knowledge and love of Christ, then our life and our words will radiate the Gospel. We should expect that each priest feels like Saint Paul: "I have no reason for boasting when I preach the Gospel; I can claim no credit for it; I cannot help myself; it would be misery to me not to preach" (1 Cor 9: 16). Unless the proclamation of the Good News is, first of all, a matter of gratitude and joy, we have understood nothing about our priesthood. And if we do not experience this, then the laity come to the same outlook.

The evangelist John, in the introduction to his first letter, magnificently expresses this dimension of evangelization: "It was there from the beginning; we have heard it; we have seen it with our own eyes; we looked upon it and felt it with our own hands; and it is of this we tell. Our theme is the word of life. This life was made visible; we have seen it and bear our testimony; we here declare to you the eternal life which dwelt with the Father and was made visible to us. What we have seen and heard we declare to you, so that you and we together may share in a common life, that life which we share with the Father and his Son Jesus Christ. And we write this in order that the joy of us all may be complete" (1 Jn 1:1-4).

We did not, like John, see Christ in his earthly life. We did not touch his glorious wounds. However, if we live in a vital faith-community and gratefully celebrate the Eucharist, living generously what we celebrate, the Holy Spirit will interiorize in us ever more the mystery of Christ. Whether we are priests or lay people, we then will become evangelists, each of us a living Gospel. The crisis of evangelization does not come from a scarcity of priests but from those — priests and others — who are able to teach abstract doctrines (and are being paid for it) while they do not know what it is to share, with heartfelt joy and gratitude, their faith-experience. This is not said to accuse these hard-working "teachers of doctrines", but as an appeal to pray and to cooperate in building up true faith-communities, and to learn together how, in the Eucharist and through it, we all can become heralds of the Good News. "The word is near you: it is upon your lips and in your heart. This means the word of faith which we proclaim. If on your lips is the confession, 'Jesus is Lord', and in your heart the faith that God raised him from the dead, then you will find salvation. For the faith that leads to righteousness is in the heart, and the confession that leads to salvation is upon the lips" (Rom 10:8-10).

The homily in the Eucharist and the preaching and teaching in the Church are important. However, they will bear fruit abundantly only if the Eucharistic spirit permeates all and everything. Then we shall feel the inner and most noble need to translate all this into our life and to share everywhere the joy, the peace and strength which we have received as undeserved gifts. We shall thus walk together on the path of salvation.

We thank you, Lord Jesus Christ,
that you have come to proclaim the Good News
with your whole life,
with words and deeds,
and finally with your death and resurrection.
    We thank you for the Church, the community of faith,
especially for the saints
who live and radiate the beatitudes.
We thank you for all the priests and religious
who have left everything behind
to consecrate themselves to the service of your Gospel.
And we thank you for our parents
whom you gave us as first heralds
of the gladdening tidings.
We praise you, too, for those
who, in the midst of their simple lives,
manifest the joy of faith and are grateful for everything.
    Increase in us a joyous faith and gratitude for it,
so that, united in your love and peace,
we may bring home to all the message
that the Father has sent you,
who live and reign for ever. Amen.

7

Lord, we thank you for the gift of faith

"If any of you falls short in wisdom, he should ask God for it and it will be given him, for God is a generous giver who neither refuses nor reproaches anyone. But he must ask in faith, without a doubt in his mind; for the doubter is like a heaving sea ruffled by the wind" (Jas 1:5-6).

On all Sundays and on the Feastdays of Our Lord, we recite, or better, we sing together the Creed. Here again it is important to see the meaning of the part in the light of the whole. The entire celebration of the Eucharist is rejoicing in grateful manifestation of our common faith and fervent prayer for increase of faith: that it may become ever more radiant, and that together we may all grow in the knowledge and love of Christ and of the Father, by the power of the Holy Spirit.

The Eucharist is a most solemn renewal of our faith in its central mysteries: that the Father so loved us that he sent his only begotten Son to be our Saviour, our Peace, our Brother. We proclaim Jesus Christ, true God and true man, the incarnate solidarity of salvation. We profess that he, who took upon himself all our burdens, teaches us his law as our law to bear each other's burdens. We sing our thanksgiving for our faith in the Holy Spirit who has anointed Jesus to be the Living Gospel, who has spoken through him, the great

Prophet. He is given to us so that we may live in Christ and with Christ and become a holy people.

The Creed in the Mass can be the 'Apostolic', in its short form, or the more solemn form of the councils of Nicaea (325) and Constantinople (381). The liturgical reform allows various alternatives so that the variety of formulations may enrich our knowledge of faith and prevent the distraction which is so easily caused by constant repetition of the same words. But the content of our faith is always the same, and so infinitely rich that each time we give voice to it, we can joyously discover a new gem that gives beauty to the whole. This can be hoped for if we understand the Creed and the whole liturgy — indeed the whole Christian life — as doxology: praise and thanksgiving.

The Creed is a challenge to examine ourselves on whether our celebrations, our reading, our dialogue with others, our entertainment, desires, decisions and deeds can be offered to God as an integral part of praise in the light of the liturgy. I suggest that we should choose our reading — our periodicals, our theological literature — with this basic criterion: "Does all this increase in us the spirit of praise and thanksgiving, and that love of neighbour, that desire to work for peace and justice, that honours God, our Father?"

Almighty and all-holy God, we praise you, for in your works you reveal yourself as almighty Father of all your children. Manifest yourself in our life as the source and goal of all love. Make us holy, make us one in your love. Give us a share of your Spirit, the bond of love. *Lord, we believe; we thank you for the gift of faith.*

Almighty Father, we praise you, for from all eternity you share all your wisdom, love and might with your Word, your only begotten Son. In the midst of history you have sent him to be one of us, our brother. Send us your Spirit, that we may better know Christ whom

42

you have sent, and you, the Father, the only true God, whom he revealed.

Lord, we believe; we thank you for the gift of faith.

We praise you, Jesus Christ, for setting us free from the slavery of sin, from arrogance and lust for power. You made yourself the freest servant of all. Grant that we may always honour you by following you as servants of our brothers and sisters.

Lord, we believe; we thank you for the gift of faith.

God our Father, we praise you for having revealed yourself totally to your beloved Son and Servant, Jesus Christ, who on the cross has made visible the full extent of your love. You have raised him from the dead and made him the Lord of all creation; you have given him a name above all names. Grant that, through your Spirit, all our thoughts, words and deeds may acknowledge and praise Christ as our Lord and, with him, honour you as his Father and our Father.

Lord, we believe; we thank you for the gift of faith.

Lord Jesus Christ, we thank you for your promise to bring all things to completion, and we look forward with joyful hope to your final coming as Saviour and as judge of the living and the dead. You have taught us that you will be merciful to the merciful and will call into your eternal kingdom all who have followed you in spirit and truth. Through your Spirit, help us to discern the signs of the times and to recognize and honour you in the needs of the afflicted, the imprisoned, the hungry and all the downtrodden.

Lord, we believe; we thank you for the gift of faith.

Holy Spirit, gift of the Father and the Son, and giver of life, we adore you, we praise you and put all our trust in you. Gratefully we accept your grace as the law of our life and of all our relationships. Come, Holy Spirit, cleanse us from selfishness and fill us with your love and consolation, so that we can become a source of love, joy, peace and brotherly justice in the world. Open our minds that we may listen to the prophets through whom you continue to speak; and help us, in all decisions and all events of our life, to honour Jesus Christ, the Prophet.

Lord, we believe; we thank you for the gift of faith.

Lord, we thank you for the Church whom you call, through your word and your life-giving Spirit, to be one, to be holy, to be universal and apostolic. We praise you for your generous patience with her and with all of us. Make us gratefully discover all the good in this Church which is yours and is also ours. Through your Spirit, grant that we, her members, may wholeheartedly accept our vocation to become holy, to be one in your love and to reach out to all people so that all together we may proclaim you as Lord and, with you, praise the Father of all.

Lord, we believe; we thank you for the gift of faith.

Lord Jesus Christ, we thank you for wanting to be baptized with the crowd in the water of the Jordan, to manifest your saving solidarity which alone can free us from the solidarity of sin.

We praise you, Father, for revealing at Jesus' baptism your humble servant as your beloved Son and the Saviour of all.

Holy Spirit, we thank you for having anointed Jesus with all your gifts, to give himself wholly to the proclamation of the Good News and to embrace his baptism in the blood of the new and everlasting covenant.

Praise and thanksgiving to you, Lord Jesus Christ! You came to reveal yourself in your baptism in the water, in the Spirit and in your blood; and through baptism you made us all blood-brothers and sisters. Help us, by your Holy Spirit, to live our baptism with joy and strength, in cooperation with all people of good will, with zeal for your glory and the glory of the Father.

Lord, we believe; we thank you for the gift of faith.

Lord Jesus Christ, we adore you in the glory of your resurrection, which is the pledge of our hope. We believe in the resurrection of all, and look forward gratefully to the new heaven and new earth. Grant that, through your Holy Spirit, our hope may issue in a common commitment for a more just and humane order of life that will lead all people on the road to the fullness of faith and hope.

Lord, we believe; we thank you for the gift of faith.

Lord, you are our joy, our peace, our strength.
Grant us an ever more joyous and grateful faith. Amen.

8

The Prayer of the Faithful

"Take salvation for helmet; for sword, take that which the Spirit gives you — the words that come from God. Give yourselves wholly to prayer and entreaty; pray on every occasion in the power of the Spirit. To this end keep watch and persevere, always interceding for all God's people"

(Eph 6:17-18).

"For this reason ... we have not ceased to pray for you. We ask God that you may receive from him all wisdom and spiritual understanding for a full insight into his will, so that your manner of life may be worthy of the Lord and entirely pleasing to him. We pray that you may bear fruit in active goodness of every kind, and grow in the knowledge of God. May he strengthen you, in his glorious might, with ample power to meet whatever comes with fortitude, patience and joy, and to give thanks to the Father who has made you fit to share the heritage of God's people in the realm of light"

(Col 1:9-12).

Just as the Creed is a grateful response to the Good News, so also, from a slightly different perspective, is the following part of the Mass, the Prayer of the Faithful. There we manifest our trust in God's goodness

47

and power. The gospel and the other readings have shown us what God has in store for his people. Through trustful prayer, we open ourselves to these gifts.

Both the gospel and the Creed have reminded us that we honour the one God and Father, the one Saviour Jesus Christ, and the one Spirit, the giver of all good gifts, by an all-embracing, saving solidarity. Therefore, we offer prayers and thanksgiving for all people. "First of all, then, I urge that petitions, prayers, intercessions and thanksgiving be offered for all men" (1 Tim 2:1).

Before the offertory we, the faithful and the celebrant, "collect" our prayers; and we do well to meditate together about the kind of prayer that can truly enter into the Eucharistic sacrifice. If the Prayer of the Faithful is to be an authentic response to the Gospel, they will express our vigilance for the signs of the times, our openness to the present opportunities, and the courage to face, with the grace of God, the challenges and responsibilities in regard to the needs of others, which our role as Christians entails.

To make the Prayer of the Faithful this alert response to the Gospel and to the signs of the Lord's coming, we should from time to time meditate in groups on what we should pray for and how to offer our petitions in a way that brings them into the dimensions of the Eucharist.

We should pray for everything. This does not mean for a million things but for intentions that are all-inclusive: for our conformity with the loving will of God, for increase in faith, hope, love of God and love of neighbour, for our own total conversion and the conversion of all people. For all this we can pray with gratitude and trust, for it will be given to us if we pray, as we should, in the name of Jesus.

Equally, we should pray for the progress of peace and justice among people and nations, for they belong directly to the reign that Christ came to establish to the honour of the Father. We rightly pray for our daily bread, for our heavenly Father cares for our needs; and if we pray in the right spirit, we realize that our bread comes from the one God and Father, and that we can rejoice in it only if we are willing to share it with the needy.

The First Letter to Timothy (2:2) appeals for prayer particularly for sovereigns and for all who exercise authority, so that we may be able to live in peace and freedom. But do we also realize that this prayer presupposes our own readiness to take our share of responsibility for the election of the right persons, for constructive critique and for sound public opinion?

Prayer does not allow escapism or apathy. We pray for "the sick"; but do we care about public health or for appropriate health services for the under-privileged? Are we interested in the ethos of the healing professions? Do we visit or help our sick friends? We pray also for "the prisoners"; but do we care for a more humanizing, healing prison system? Are we ready to enter into correspondence with prisoners or visit them? We pray for "the lonely"; but do we visit any of them? Are we inventive in helping them to overcome their loneliness?

We pray frequently for the millions of people who suffer from starvation or malnutrition. Do we also realize that we can help to bring about a change? If we pray for peace and non-violent action for justice, does this increase in us the desire to become ever better peacemakers both in our own milieu and beyond it?

Each of us prays for the needs to which we are sensitive. We share our prayers of petition and thus help each other to open our hearts to many new dimensions.

We thank you, Lord,
that in your Church
and through the power of your Holy Spirit,
you teach us how and for what to pray.

49

D

Send your Spirit,
that we may pray with great trust
and with passionate love for all people,
especially those who are suffering.
Cleanse our hearts, O Lord,
so that our prayer may always be sincere. Amen.

9

Everything is sacred: God's gift

"Through Jesus, then, let us continually offer up to God the sacrifice of praise, that is, the tribute of lips which acknowledges his name, and never forget to show kindness and to share what you have with others; for such are the sacrifices which God approves" (Heb 13:15-16).

"Blessed are you, Lord, God of all creation. Through your goodness we have this bread . . . this wine to offer, fruit of the earth . . . the vine, and work of human hands. It will become for us the bread of life . . . our spritual drink".

Teilhard de Chardin liked to cry out joyously, "Everything is sacred!" In the light of the Eucharist, his life became a celebration of the cosmic liturgy, a great vision of how everything is the gift of the Creator and Redeemer and, therefore, plays a role in the history of creation and salvation.

A sober theology of secularization tells us emphatically this truth: of itself, nothing is profane. Only the sinner profanes himself and everything he touches with selfish arrogance, by refusing to honour God, the source of all things. Where there is no gratitude, the gifts of God are lost. "Do not deceive yourselves, my friends. All good giving and every perfect gift comes from above, from the Father of the lights of heaven.

With him there is no variation, no play of passing shadows" (Jas 1:16-17).

To live without gratitude means to imprison oneself in darkness, miserableness, self-deception. Inevitably, ungrateful people become manipulated manipulators. But for those who are fully conscious that everything is a gift of the one God and Father, this grateful knowledge becomes the leitmotif and basic criterion for their lives. They live in the light of truth, in dignity and freedom, creating a truly divine milieu wherever they are.

Bread and wine are, by their God-given nature, symbols of unity. The many grains become one loaf; the many grapes yield the wine. As gifts of the one Father, they unite the family around the table, and friends and even strangers will be welcomed there. The grateful receiver of the bread knows that his own capacities, his intelligence and labour come also from God. Thus, everything calls him to ever greater solidarity with his whole environment and with all people.

For the ungrateful, the bread and wine become a source of division, distrust, envy, quarrels, wars. Everyone seeks his own bigger piece: two beefsteaks while others are starving. Each is fighting for *his* privileges, *his* freedoms, while denying the dignity and freedom of others. They thus undermine their own dignity which they base on their colour, their wealth, their power of office, their social status — their selfishness. About the nature of real freedom, real dignity, and about the nature of bread, wine and all the other things, they are abysmally ignorant.

The Eucharist can bring about the great change: the wonderful consecration of all earthly reality. If we so celebrate the Eucharist that it becomes the form and norm of our life, we discover the beautiful nature of the bread, the wine, of our liberty, our individuality, and of all we have in common. We become effective messengers in a saving solidarity of justice, peace, unity.

And the more we commit ourselves to this vision, the more truthfully and joyfully will we celebrate the Eucharist as the sacrament of unity.

We cannot, however, ignore the fact that today we have to celebrate the Eucharist in a divided Christianity and a divided world. We offer the bread and wine in a society in which Christians waste an enormous portion of our earth's resources while millions of people suffer from all kinds of under-development. And we should feel humiliated that Christians, while neglecting the integral knowledge of Christ, not only take unjust divisions of the earth's goods but often use the words of the Bible and half-truths of our faith to fight against each other for these things: all because of lack of gratitude to God upon whom we are all totally dependent.

If we are to celebrate the Eucharist as an effective sign of unity, we need a manifold conversion and recon-ciliation. We have to reconcile ourselves with the true meaning of bread, wine, and all earthly things includ-ing our capacities, so that they become again what they were meant to be: signs of solidarity before God, the giver of all good things. But all this is possible only if we reconcile ourselves with God in and through the Eucharist, in a gratitude so deeply felt that we truly offer ourselves and all that we are and all that we have to God in the service of our fellowmen.

It is self-evident that this grateful reconciliation with God, with ourselves and with the gifts of God can only happen if we are reconciled with all of God's children. "If, when you are bringing your gift to the altar, you suddenly remember that your brother has a grievance against you, leave your gift where it is before the altar. First go and make your peace with your brother, and only then come back and offer your gift" (Mt 5:23-24).

The book of Genesis discloses God's original design for basic human relationships. Adam — **man** —

receives Eve — woman — with great joy as a gift from God. They honour each other as equals: both woman and man are recognized as image of God. As long as they adore God and render thanks in mutual appreciation, their life is a paradise. But as soon as they become self-important and refuse to honour God as God (cf Rom 1:21ff) they become a threat to each other, despise and accuse each other. They thus drive themselves out of paradise.

Reconciliation happens only in the radical conversion to the truth that everything and everyone is a gift of God. We can offer our gifts and ourselves in the Eucharist only in this ever-present gratitude that opens us to our fellowmen, lets us appreciate all their goodness and makes us ready to serve them. God admonishes us through the prophet. "When you come in to visit me, who asks these things of you? Trample my courts no more! Bring no more worthless offerings; your incense is loathsome to me. New moon and Sabbath, calling of assemblies, octaves with wickedness: these I cannot bear. Your new moons and festivals I detest; they weigh me down, I tire of the load. When you spread out your hands, I close my eyes to you; though you pray the more, I will not listen. Your hands are full of blood! Wash yourselves clean! Put away your misdeeds from my eyes; cease doing evil; learn to do good. Make justice your aim; redress the wronged, hear the orphan's plea, defend the widow. Come now, let us set things right, says the Lord: though your sins be like scarlet" (Is 1:12-18).

The truthful celebration of the Eucharist is very demanding. It means uniting ourselves totally with Christ who has offered himself even to the point of shedding his blood for us in an everlasting blood-covenant. He has thus honoured the Father and prepared redemption for us. And since God the Father has given us everything in his Son, we can respond to this infinite love only with the freest, most joyful and

grateful sacrifice. "Each person should give as he has
decided for himself; there should be no reluctance,
no sense of compulsion; God loves a cheerful giver"
(2 Cor 9:7).

God blames those Israelites who bring for sacrifice
only sick and blind or lame animals, and sigh when
they offer them. "But you behave profanely towards
me by thinking the Lord's table and its offering may
be polluted and its food slighted. You also say, 'What
a burden!' and you scorn it, says the Lord of hosts.
'You bring in what you seize, or the lame or the sick,
yes, you bring it as a sacrifice. Shall I accept it from
your hands?' says the Lord" (Mal 1:12-13). Against
this sad background the prophet foretells the new era,
that of the Eucharistic sacrifice: "For, from the rising
of the sun even to its setting, my name is great among
the nations; and everywhere they bring sacrifice to my
name and a pure offering; for great is my name among
the nations, says the Lord of hosts" (Mal 1:11).

When we think about the tremendous honour of
belonging to Christ and his prophetic priesthood, we
can offer ourselves only with such thankfulness and
joy that every renunciation becomes light. As living
stones, we form the temple of the Holy Spirit, consecrated to God and offered as a spiritual sacrifice accepted
by God through Jesus Christ (cf. 1 Pet 2:5). We are
authentically a "spiritual sacrifice" offered and sancti-
fied by the Holy Spirit if we recognize and treat
everything as a gift of God who gives all good gifts and
unifies all people. Leaving behind our selfish self, we
find our real self in the truth.

Twenty years ago, some dioceses in the United States
promoted tithing with the slogan, "10% for God,
90% for yourself". The Eucharist tells us, "100% for
God". Anything else is a bad bargain. We shall use
all our talents and all our earthly goods in the service
of his Kingdom, through whatever channels are open
to us. That means that we shall serve our fellowmen,

our Church, families, communities and our whole
environment, in accordance with the Eucharistic truth:
Everything is sacred, a gift of God.

Father, we are yours,
for all and everything is your gift.
We thank you, and ask you to help us
to give to you our total gratitude
as you have given us everything in Jesus Christ.
  Lord, send us your Holy Spirit,
that we may deeply sense
that everything is sacred
and calls for a life of praise and gratitude.
Help us to honour your name
by a generous use of all your gifts.
Grant that we may always realize our dependence on you
and, therefore, share everything
with our brothers and sisters
to your glory. Through Christ our Lord.
Amen.

10

To render thanks always:
the way to salvation

"For since it was a man who brought death into the world, a man also brought resurrection of the dead. As in Adam all men die, so in Christ all will be brought to life; but each in his own proper place: Christ the first-fruits, and afterwards, at his coming, those who belong to Christ. Then comes the end when he delivers up the kingdom of God the Father, after abolishing every kind of domination, authority and power. For he is destined to reign until God has put all enemies under his feet; and the last enemy to be abolished is death. Scripture says, 'He has put all things in subjection under his feet'. But in saying 'all things', it clearly means to exclude God who subordinates them; and when all things are thus subject to him, then the Son himself will also be made subordinate to God who made all things subject to him, and thus God will be all in all" (1 Cor 15:21-28).

With our "Holy, Holy, Holy", joining the song of the angels and saints we come to the very heart of the Eucharist. Again, priest and participants bless each other, "The Lord be with you" — "And also with you". "Lift up your hearts!" Listening to the word of God, offering ourselves as a gift coming from God, and filled with humility and thanksgiving, we have lifted up our hearts.

As we have seen, the Eucharist, in all its parts, is thanksgiving. But now there is a solemn appeal: "Let us give thanks to the Lord our God!" And the participants express their readiness to enter into the deepest and highest dimension of thanksgiving. "It is right and fitting — it is our delightful duty — it is the way to wholeness and salvation — to give thanks always and everywhere!" In view of the memorial of the suffering and death of Christ, nothing can be excepted. Christ, who has suffered and died for us, leads the heavenly liturgy. We look to him: how he gave thanks while he took the cup of salvation, when he prepared himself to drink to the last drop the chalice of suffering for us.

Suffering and death, as sinful humankind experiences them, are not good. They manifest a disordered world and can drive people into despair and rebellion. They are poisoned by man's sin, his alienation from God, his lack of gratitude, his self-centredness and falsehood.

Christ did not bring suffering and death into the world but he gave them a new meaning. He did not suffer and die for himself but for us, and thereby made these most miserable fates in the world — suffering and death — the greatest signs of his freedom to love. Freely he takes upon himself our burden, and freely he entrusts his spirit, his life, into the Father's hands. He knows that the Father will raise him from death.

Even in view of past sins and their consequences we can give thanks, for they have found such a Saviour. In union with Christ's suffering, through our heartfelt contrition, we detest our sins and can give to the past a new shape. We are not condemned to the slavery of sin.

If we accept the Easter mystery as the norm of our morality, then we know that, through suffering, we can grow in spiritual maturity and have a share in Christ's redeeming action. With St Paul we can say,

"It is now my happiness to suffer for you. This is my way of helping to complete, in my poor human flesh, the full tale of Christ's afflictions still to be endured, for the sake of his body which is the Church" (Col 1:24).

Now, senseless suffering yields its place to compassion. Christ's suffering, freely offered for us, has shown that the Father in heaven is a compassionate God. This is the breathtaking message: the all-holy God is with us; he is not indifferent to human misery; he is truly involved in shaping our history. And from that, the commandment of love receives this new dimension: "Be compassionate as your Father is compassionate" (Lk 6:36).

If, with Christ, we praise the compassionate love of the heavenly Father by accepting suffering and death as an expression of saving solidarity with and for our brothers and sisters, we are growing towards our full stature in Christ. We are following him who, in his extreme suffering on the cross, was full of concern not only for his holy mother and the beloved disciple but also for the thief who was crucified with him to humiliate him. He makes the thief his friend; and he prays for those who crucify him. His heart goes out to all.

It is in profound gratitude to Christ that we see our own troubles, turmoils and sufferings in the right perspective. For me, a central message, worthy to be shared with others, is that whoever accepts his suffering and brings it home into the thanksgiving with which Christ took the chalice of salvation can be sure that he possesses an authentic relic of Christ's cross, a share in his salvific death. I said this once to a gentleman who showed me an official document assuring him that the little piece of wood he had was an authentic relic of the cross. He wanted to be sure that there could be no doubt about it. I expressed my opinion that even the Pope could not assure him of this, but that if he would thank the Lord because his sufferings are redeemed and redeeming, and thus gratefully accept them, then he could be infallibly sure that he possessed an authentic relic of the true cross. Very happily he responded, "This makes sense!"

We shall fight suffering in the world as far as we can. As Christians, we are especially obliged to fight against all those forms of suffering that are inflicted by sinful people on their neighbours: against injustice, hatred, contempt and the like. But we embrace those forms of sacrifice, self-denial, conflict and suffering necessary for the fulfilment of the great law of Christ, "Love one another as I have loved you" (Jn 15:12).

We shall fight against sin, which is the source of all evil. In this battle we cannot spare ourselves and others the sorrow, affliction and pain necessary for conversion. That conversion is necessary is a saddening fact, but that it is possible is a primary reason to praise the Lord.

Our gratitude for Christ's suffering for us provides the impulse to fight injustice and unjustly inflicted suffering. At the same time we shall try to help people, by example and word, to understand the challenge of suffering and how, through the Eucharistic power and spirit, everything can be transfigured. Gratitude, mutual appreciation, all the manifestations of saving solidarity are forces of transfiguration in which Christ's death and resurrection are operative.

In an advice-column in a magazine, in response to a letter from a young lady suffering from a genetic disease, who strongly proposed abortion for the prevention of these forms of life-long suffering, I wrote the story of Michael and John, two young friends of mine. Both are afflicted by genetic diseases far heavier than the young lady's, yet they consider themselves among the most privileged people in the world, for they have received from their parents so much love and a deep faith that gives meaning to their lives. The unhappy girl, in a following letter, repeated her conviction that, for her, it would have been better if her parents had resolved the problem by abortion. Thus the meaning of her suffering was, time and again, aborted.

Answering her second letter, I noted that nobody has a right to judge the despairing, for we do not know who bears the guilt. Perhaps nobody had helped the sick girl to understand the meaning of all this. It was a very moving experience for me, however, to receive a number of letters from people who had suffered during a long life, had given it meaning, and wanted to enter into friendly contact with the desperate girl in order to share with her their faith-experience. What a difference between suffering "that makes sense" and suffering without meaning! Happy are those who perceive the consecrating power of Christ's death and resurrection. When all our life gives praise to God, the Eucharist leads us ever deeper into this transfiguration.

To want to eliminate suffering by means as cruel as abortion will only increase unredeemed and desperate pain. They increase the very source of the worst evils in the world. Those who refuse the message and power of the Paschal Mystery and the invitation to make their life a thanksgiving with Christ will always find reasons to curse their fate. And whatever may be their earthly achievements, they find the ultimate limit in death which will inevitably confront them with God whom they have treated not as a bountiful Father but as a threat.

For those, however, who have entered into the Eucharistic dimension by constant thanksgiving and mutual appreciation, and in a living faith, the whole life-experience is different. And when death approaches, they can, with St Francis, greet it as a beloved sister, as the gracious coming of the Lord, the final home-coming. For them, death will never mean the last and final loss, the summit of senselessness, the help-

less rebellion, but rather the hour of the final transfiguration, of trust and peace. "How great was my
joy as I was told, 'We go to the house of the Lord' "
(Ps 121).

Father, all-powerful and ever-living God,
we do well always and everywhere to give you thanks.
You have no need of our praise,
yet our desire to thank you is itself your gift.
Our prayer of thanksgiving
adds nothing to your greatness,
but makes us grow in your grace,
through Christ our Lord.
Amen.

11

A grateful memory

"I remember the deeds of the Lord; yes, I remember your wonders of old. And I meditate on your works; your exploits I ponder. O God, your way is holy; what great god is there like our God? You are the God who works wonders; among the people you have made known your power" (Ps 77:11-15).

Another name of the Eucharist that calls us to gratitude is "Memorial of the death, resurrection and ascension of the Lord". A "memorial" recalls a memory. The Eucharist makes present to us the great event of the history of salvation. But it is infinitely more than a matter of memory; it is the real presence of the Lord that gives to the here-and-now a burning intensity. The Lord himself, in his gracious presence is reminding us about all that he has done for us and reassuring us of his promises.

Yet it is clear that all this will not transform us if it does not touch our memory. St Augustine rightly gave great importance to the human memory. Without it we would not truly live history. It is the precious endowment that gives us conscious continuity and a liberating transition from the past to the future. Therefore, a vital question for us is: what kind of a memory do we have? Is it healthy or sick — or insane? Has it depth or is it a realm of superficiality?

Superficial people swim in the present and are driven by it; but they do not experience it in its deeply human sense, for they do not bring home to it the wealth of the past and cannot, therefore, transmit it to the future with a clear direction. Their own presence is thereby confused and impoverished.

There are people who have tenacious but sick — and sometimes insane — memories. They constantly awaken the dark and hostile events of the past that can only perpetuate wounds, frictions, misunderstandings, hatred and enmities. They work destruction. People with this kind of memory will discover everywhere the negative side. Suspicious and judgmental, they become gradually unable to trust, to rejoice, to love. These people are poorly prepared to celebrate the Eucharist and show that they draw little profit from it.

If our memory is enriched and marked by the grateful celebration of all that the Lord has done for us in creation, in his incarnation, death and resurrection, then our memory will be healed and filled with a stream of redemptive remembrances. These remembrances, and thankfulness for them, will shed their light on everything in our past, our present, and in our outlook on the future. When we gladly remember all the good we have received and experienced throughout our life, we learn to look always first for the good in our neighbour and in ourselves. We thus come to see our past experiences, even our sufferings and misunderstandings in the right light, in a healing perspective.

This does not imply that we are blind to the evil, sin and suffering of the past and of the present hour. Rather, we find the freedom and courage to face these sides of life, thanks to the spirit of thanksgiving and praise. We have established a decent balance in which the dark powers appear relatively small in comparison with the gifts and the goodness of God. When others offend us or misinterpret our actions, words and intentions, our memory will immediately remind us how graciously God has forgiven us, how patiently he purifies our motives. Then it will be almost natural that we, too, will show healing forgiveness to those who have grieved us.

The favoured and most striking moment of a grateful memory is in the celebation of the Eucharist, when the Lord makes himself present not only in his word but also especially in his glorified body. The "visit to the Blessed Sacrament" has also a special grace for our memory when we repose quietly before the Lord, recalling his goodness, counting his blessings, and thus preparing ourselves for the next celebration. We also adore Jesus in his attentiveness to the sick and suffering, and thus become more vigilant for the various ways he sometimes visits and calls us.

The Eucharistic presence includes and illumines the past and the future. The wonderful events and gifts of the past reach and enrich us through a grateful memory. Hope opens the horizons of the future, and lives and thrives, from the memory's storehouse. Hope is praise for God's promises and leads to a firm commitment of fidelity. Between the past and the future, the grateful memory calls for vigilance and action in the here-and-now and openness to the future.

These are the three main dimensions of the eschatological virtues: gratitude, vigilance, hope. They engender discernment and serenity. More than anything else, it is the grateful memory that lends its energies to these virtues and allows that serenity without which discernment is not possible.

These eschatological virtues are more basic than the classical (Greek) "cardinal virtues", since they include those virtues and give them the dimension of the history of salvation, without which we could not understand the specifically Christian dimensions of faith and charity. They are not static but dynamic.

A grateful memory will never allow us complacency

or laziness. It will encourage and even impel us to continue on the road of ongoing conversion and of renewal in Church and society.

Merciful Father,
we have sinned by our superficiality
and by a distracted life,
and, worse, we have damaged our memory
by filling it with worrisome and angry remembrances.
Heal us, Lord.
Grant us a grateful memory,
that we may worthily celebrate the Eucharist
and open ourselves to its grace.
Let us remember through all our life,
especially in the moments of grave decisions,
the innumerable signs of your love,
the incarnation, life and death,
resurrection and ascension
of your Son, Jesus Christ.
We thank you for the mission of the Holy Spirit
who heals our memory
and makes us vigilant for the final coming of your Son
and for every opportunity to serve you.
Lord, make us grateful,
through Christ our Lord.
Amen.

12

One in Christ, to the glory
of God the Father

"Form your own judgment on what I say. When
we bless 'the cup of blessing', is it not a means
of sharing in the blood of Christ? When we break
the bread, is it not a means of sharing in the body
of Christ? Because there is one loaf, we, many as
we are, are one body, for it is one loaf of which
we all partake" (1 Cor 10:16-17).

With St Augustine, the Second Vatican Council calls
the Memorial of Christ's death and resurrection "a
sacrament of love, a sign of unity, a bond of charity"
(Constitution on the Sacred Liturgy, 47). The same
truth is emphasized by St Paul's text quoted above.
We cannot eat the body of Christ, drink from the chalice
of his blood, and offer the Eucharistic sacrifice to the
Father, in the Holy Spirit, without joining in the great
Eucharistic prayer of Christ for unity. The commitment to
saving solidarity, to unity and peace, is an essential part
of the grace of the Eucharist and of our thanksgiving.
When we receive the body of Christ fruitfully, we accept
our vocation to become worthy members of his body.

In Christ, the Word Incarnate, the Father has given
us everything, since from all eternity he shares all his
wisdom, love, beauty and power in and with his Word.
The Father's greatest and all-embracing gift to his
creation is the hypostatic union with his eternal Word,
given to Jesus of Nazareth. And Jesus is gratefully
aware that he has received this unique privilege in

view of all humanity — indeed, in view of the whole creation. His thanksgiving to the Father, is, therefore, also an expression of his brotherhood with all people, of total dedication to share the Good News with humankind, and to call all to unity in adoration of the one God and Father.

This dedication to unity receives its loftiest expression when, on the cross, Jesus stretches out his arms and opens his heart to everyone. In response, our praise and thanksgiving issues in commitment to this solidarity of salvation, to unity in Christ to the praise of God, the Father of all.

The mystery of the inseparable synthesis between thanksgiving and the service of unity is wonderfully expressed in the high-priestly prayer of Jesus (Jn 17). The only begotten Son reveals the glory of the Father by offering himself "that all may be one". By the hypostatic union and through the fullness of the Holy Spirit, Jesus is consecrated to do the costly work of unity; and we shall never enter into these dimensions if, ungratefully, we forget the price — the precious blood of Christ, the blood of the new and everlasting covenant.

We are entrusted to him by the Father. Returning to the Father, he prays for us that we, too, may be consecrated in truth to the same work, in the same spirit of sacrifice. "Holy Father, protect, by the power of thy name, those whom thou hast given me, that they may be one, as we are one" (Jn 17:11).

When Christ calls us to discipleship and friendship with himself, he calls us to share in his unity with the Father through the gift of the Spirit who alone can consecrate us to the task of unity and peace. Those privileged disciples who celebrate and live the Eucharist intensely, with that gratitude in which Christ offered himself to the Father as a living Gospel and as call to unity, will give that witness of cordial love and harmonious interaction that becomes a sign, grace and call to unity for all people.

Grateful faith makes the prayer of Jesus our programme of life: "I pray also for those who, through their words, put their faith in me; may they all be one: as thou, Father, art in me and I in thee, so also may they be in us, that the world may believe that thou didst send me. The glory which thou gavest me I have given to them, that they may be one as we are one; I in them and thou in me, may they be perfectly one. Then the world will learn that thou didst send me, that thou didst love them as thou didst me" (Jn 17:21-23).

When we are gathered around Christ, we eat from him who gives himself as the bread of unity and drink from the one cup of the everlasting covenant. Here the oneness is already realized, not only symbolically but through our real union with Christ and among ourselves. We are united with the choirs of angels and saints in Christ, the head of all creation, and have a share in the heavenly liturgy. All this gives us the impulse and strength to live ever better the saving solidarity to which Christ calls us. Willing to bear each other's burdens and to honour each other as members of God's family, we experience an ever-increasing gratitude to Christ, the great Sacrament of unity.

The concelebration by the priests with the active participation of all the faithful symbolizes this oneness and solidarity. But we should not forget that we concelebrate Christ's sacrifice and we should, therefore, understand that our endeavours for unity, as praise of the Father with Christ, requires daily self-denial.

When we say, "Hallowed be thy name", we adore and pray to the Father "in spirit and truth" if there is in us a burning desire to make the name of the one God and Father known to all through our mutual love and unity — "that the world may believe". We work, then, for the unity of humankind, that all may visibly and truly belong to the new family which Christ is calling together.

The kingdom of God is already manifested on earth

wherever Christ's disciples, guided by God's gifts, join their talents, their possessions and energies to build a more just and humane world and to promote, patiently and courageously, not only Christian unity but the unity of all the children of God.

If we are truly inspired by that gratitude which the Eucharist teaches us, our prayer, "Thy will be done on earth as it is in heaven", will be authentic and fruitful. We will discover how the various charisms can be brought together for the benefit of all, in unity and charity. We shall seek together to fulfil the will of the Father that, through our saving solidarity, all may be freed from the solidarity of perdition. We can then truthfully pray that we may not succumb to temptation and be delivered from evil.

When we eat the Bread of Life and drink the Cup of Salvation, we offer as our thanksgiving our vow to practice and to work for unity in faith, hope, charity and justice. "How shall I make a return to the Lord for all the good he has done for me? The cup of salvation I will take up, and I will call upon the name of the Lord. My vows to the Lord I will pay in the presence of his people" (Ps 116:12-14).

Father almighty,
fill our hearts and memories with that gratitude
which inspired your beloved Son Jesus
to consecrate himself totally to his mission,
to call all people together
through the gospel of love and peace
and through his death on the cross.
Grant to your people abundant grace of the Holy Spirit,
so that the joyous and grateful celebration
of the greatest sign of unity, the Eucharist,
may become clear vision and strength
for our dedication to unity and peace.
Through Christ our Lord.
Amen.

13

In communion with all the Church

"Remember your leaders, those who first spoke God's message to you; and reflecting upon the outcome of their life and work, follow the example of their faith. Jesus Christ is the same yesterday, today and for ever" (Heb 13:7-8).

To belong to God's great family is the greatest joy and honour. In the Eucharist, we remember gratefully all the family members. We turn our attention to the saints in heaven, to all who are still with us on this earthly pilgrimage, to those who, in purgatory, are longing to enter fully into their inheritance.

In the first Eucharistic Prayer (the traditional Roman Canon), we pray, before the consecration, for the whole Church, for her unity and peace, for the pope, for our bishop and for all who profess the faith transmitted by the apostles. There is no other way, of course, to keep the faith pure than to live and transmit it as the Good News. We then pray for those present around us whose faith and devotion is known to God: a beautiful expression of reverence. The priest reminds all that they, too, offer this sacrifice of praise and that we offer prayers for all those who are dear to us. Since we are disciples of Christ, even our enemies are dear to us. We bless them and pray for them, although we may think first of those who are closest to us.

All together, then, we gratefully remember and honour Mary, the mother of our Lord Jesus Christ and our mother. We remember St Joseph, the apostles, martyrs and all the saints. We are one family with them and know that their merits and prayers are present for us.

In the other (new) Eucharistic Prayers, the special remembrance of the saints takes place after the consecration. They are with us and we with them during the whole celebration and, indeed, throughout our whole life. The saints are in the glory of God, totally transformed in praise and thanksgiving. They are in Christ, and the more we live in and with Christ, the more intimate is our union and saving solidarity with them.

We remember especially those who have gone before us marked with the sign of faith. We thus respond to the exhortation in the Letter to the Hebrews (13:7): "Remember those who have guided you and have announced to you the word of God". In all African and many other ancient cultures, the common remembrance of their forefathers, of all the members of the family and clan or tribe who have died, is of great religious and moral significance. These religious people are convinced that the dead continue their interest in whether their descendants and friends remember them and — most important — whether, in consequence, they honour them by the way they live, by observance of the good traditions, the family spirit, by justice and generosity. They would not be fully happy in the assembly of the ancestors if their offspring were forgetful and dishonoured them by an immoral life. · Hence, the grateful remembrance of those who have transmitted not only life but also moral standards is a central theme which cannot be neglected without great damage.

There is nothing superstitious in this basic vision, although there is always some danger when such ingredients enter. By its very nature, this remembrance comes to fulfillment in the Eucharist, and Christians should observe, not less but even more, these dynamic dimensions that guarantee the synthesis between religious celebration and our everyday life.

Gratitude obliges us to pray for those in purgatory; but our intercession must be well integrated in the mystery of a solidarity of salvation, of which the Eucharist is the most sublime, rewarding and demanding expression.

The doctrine of the Church on the offering of the Mass for the dead, and on indulgences for the living and the dead, has to be seen in this light. It will benefit those who have lived or live now in accordance with the grace and task of solidarity in Christ. There is no indulgence for selfishness or for a self-centred individualism. Our individual salvation is included in and guaranteed by the solidary salvation and the shared praise of God.

O Lord, what an honour and joy
to share life with you and the Father in the Holy Spirit,
and to belong to your wonderful family:
those in heaven, those on earth, those in purgatory.
Let our faith in the communion of saints
issue in genuine communication,
so that the memorial of the saints
may make us more generous in our sharing on earth and
in our readiness to bear a part of the burden of others.
Let the remembrance of the dead become
a moral force for Christians
even more than for those of the ancient religions.
Glorify your name in your all-embracing family
by converting us totally to solidarity of salvation.
Amen.

14

Prayer: joyous, grateful response

"At that moment Jesus exulted in the Holy Spirit and said, 'I thank thee, Father, Lord of heaven and earth, for hiding these things from the learned and wise and revealing them to the simple. Yes, Father, such was thy creation'. Then turning to his disciples he said, 'Everything is entrusted to me by my Father; and no one knows who the Son is but the Father, or who the Father is but the Son, and those to whom the Son may choose to reveal him'.

"Turning to his disciples in private he said, 'Happy the eyes that see what you are seeing! I tell you, many prophets and kings wished to see what you now see, yet never saw it; to hear what you hear, yet never heard it" (Lk 10:21-24).

We remind ourselves again that in each part of the Eucharistic celebration the whole picture is present and operative and, therefore, each part enriches our vision of the beauty and wealth of the whole. This is particularly true of the Lord's Prayer when it follows the great doxology, "through him, with him, in him, in the unity of the Holy Spirit, all glory and honour is yours almighty Father, for ever and ever. Amen".

We sing this song of praise in thankful awareness that all blessings and all good things are given us in Christ. Then we pray — or better, sing — the "Our

Father" in preparation for communion, which will enable us ever more to sing with Christ the praise of the Father.

All prayers should be understood as thanksgiving in response to God's active word. We first listen to God and look at all he has done and revealed for us. We can be sure that God listens to our good prayers, but we have to add that our prayer is not good unless we have first listened to him and gratefully meditated on his works and his gifts.

We do well also to meditate on the "Our Father" in the light of Jesus' exultant words quoted above. Our prayer is joyful because the Father has revealed to us his love in Jesus, and Jesus proclaims the Good News that we can go with him to the Father. How can we not rejoice when we hear Jesus' jubilant cry, "Abba!", "Dear Father", in his joy that his disciples have come to that deep knowledge of the mystery of salvation that allows them to share in the proclamation of the Good News? And what greater joy could Jesus share with us than our new birthright as children of God, to call his Father "our Father"? "But to all who did receive him, to those who have yielded him their allegiance, he gave the right to become children of God . . ." (Jn 1:12).

This birthright is supremely exercised when we are invited to the Lord's Supper to share his body and blood. Gratitude discovers there the dimensions of the family of God. Our rejoicing before the Father becomes also fraternal love and zeal to bring all people home into the same joy and gift in the unity of faith.

The Eucharist discloses to us how wonderfully God has glorified his name "Father" in his beloved Son and in those who wholeheartedly follow him in prayer and life. Our grateful response is a burning desire to honour our Father as his true children, by a universal love and justice, and in the proclamation of the Gospel, so that all may join in adoration of the one true God, the Father of our Lord Jesus Christ.

By the power of the Holy Spirit, the Father has taken total hold of Jesus who, as servant of God and man, makes known the dimensions of God's kingdom. Our response is a great longing to let God truly be God in every area of our life. Since he guides us by his Spirit and by all the marvellous signs of his love, we pray that he may completely mould us too, filling us with faith, trust, hope and generosity. Then our gratitude will make all of God's gifts fruitful to us; we shall build up that unity, justice and that divine milieu of mutual appreciation and encouragement that makes visible the coming of the kingdom. Our acts will never stem from fear but only from that divine love that alone can unite us to the honour of the loving Father of all.

In the presence of the risen Lord, we praise the Father for having sent us Jesus to do his compassionate will on this earth "as it is in heaven", in God's own life and in the assembly of the angels and saints. Whoever knows Jesus knows the will of the Father. We pray thankfully for a better knowledge of Jesus and of the Father. We pray that we may be filled by the Holy Spirit so that we shall seek nothing else than to conform with the will of God and give convincing witness through which others may come to know and love his will and unite in his praise.

In the Eucharist we pray for the gift of bread while the Bread of Life is already prepared for the banquet. Our prayer recognizes, above all, that all this is an absolutely undeserved gift. As we open ourselves, then, to the Bread that lasts forever, we also realize that our daily bread is given by the one Father, and we pray that we may use it in such a way that all may recognize the Giver.

Reassured of God's mercy after the confession of our sins to the praise of God's mercy, we pray that we may become instruments and signs of God's healing forgiveness; that, reconciled with God, we may always act as reconcilers.

Whoever has experienced the beatitude and strength that comes from a vital Eucharistic community can face the threats of a sinful environment. Gratefully united in Christ, we pray that we may create communities and build up public opinions and social, economic, cultural and political structures that do not lead people into temptation but, rather, help them in their growth towards maturity and commitment to justice. Whoever is seized by the power of God's kingdom and filled with gratitude will not be discouraged. We shall therefore work patiently and creatively for the victory of God's goodness in our world. Hence, our prayer "Lead us not into temptation but deliver us from evil" is an expression of trust. It opens us to the grace of working faithfully for God's kingdom. The Eucharistic character which is gradually formed by all this provides the necessary strength and endurance.

In the *Didaché* (Doctrine of the Twelve Apostles, written around 46 A.D.), the Lord's Prayer ends with the well-known praise, "For thine is the kingdom, the power and the glory, now and forever". Eminent biblical scholars explain that this praise is not contained in the formulations of Matthew and Luke because, in early Christianity, everyone, even in community, concluded the prayer with praise, and great room was left for spontaneity. Here is a creative note from which we can learn. As the liturgical renewal of the Second Vatican Council comes to its full beauty, there will surely be a better understanding about this dimension of creativity and the dynamics of prayer.

We thank you, Lord Jesus,
for teaching us how to pray
and for continuing to lead our prayer.
We thank you especially
for your presence in the Eucharist
that gives to our prayer great joy and trust.

Send your Holy Spirit, that we may cry out
in us and through us
"Abba! Dear Father!"
Increase in us faith, hope and love,
so that all our prayer and life
may become a joyous and generous response
to you, the living Gospel,
and united with you, to the Father.
Amen.

15

The gift of peace

"Then, put on the garments that suit God's chosen people, his own, his beloved: compassion, kindness, humility, gentleness, patience. Be forbearing with one another, and forgiving where any of you has cause for complaint; you must forgive as the Lord forgave you. To crown all, there must be love to bind all together and complete the whole. Let Christ's peace be arbiter in your hearts" (Col 3:12-15).

Singing the "Our Father", the privileged prayer of the sons and daughters of God, should remind us that only those who spread the peace of Christ are sure to be called children of God. "Blessed are the peacemakers; God will call them his children" (Mt 5:9).

Before going to suffer for us, Jesus promised his disciples the fullness of messianic peace. "Peace is my parting gift to you, my own peace such as the world cannot give. Set your troubled hearts at rest and banish your fears" (Jn 14:27). And the first greeting that the risen Lord shares with them is "Peace be with you!". Having then shown his pierced hands and side to the disciples, who were "filled with joy" at seeing him, "Jesus repeated, 'Peace be with you!' As the Father has sent me, so I send you. He then breathed on them, saying, 'Receive the Holy Spirit! If you forgive any man's sins they stand forgiven; if you pronounce them unforgiven, unforgiven they remain!" (Jn 20:20-23). Thus he makes them sharers and messengers of his peace.

In preparation for Communion, it is impossible to overlook the centrality of the message of peace and the prayer for peace immediately following the "Our Father". In these prayers we implore peace for ourselves, for the Church and for all the world. The celebrant and the people bless each other in Christ's peace, and with the kiss of peace they recommit themselves to be peacemakers. Communion is the kiss of peace we receive from Christ, who gives us himself and, thus, the fullness of peace.

It is important to see clearly the Eucharistic dimension of messianic peace. Paul speaks of it insistently, greeting all the churches with "Grace and peace from God the Father and our Lord Jesus Christ". He asks that they "live at peace with all men" (Rom 12:18) and "Greet one another with the kiss of peace" (Rom 16:16). He tells the Colossians, "In this peace you are called as members of a single body. And be filled with gratitude" (3:15). His wish for the Thessalonians is, "May the Lord of peace himself give you peace at all times and in all ways" (2 Thess 3:16).

We must, first of all, see the peace of Christ as an undeserved gift prepared by the suffering and death of Christ, shared with us by the risen Lord. It can, therefore, be received only by grateful people. The second dimension is that of solidarity: the gift of the one Lord *for all*. Whoever is truly grateful will share this peace with others and cooperate with others to work for peace at all times and everywhere. Those who lose this peace of heart not only sin against themselves but deprive their whole environment of its precious good.

Gratitude and co-responsibility, if they take deep roots in us, will reward us with self-control, serenity and peace. Nothing in this world, not even abuse and defamation, is in any proportion to the peace of Christ who entrusts to us the task of being artisans of the kingdom of peace.

Christ's peace becomes, through gratitude, a permanent mission. "Go in peace", or "Go in the peace of Christ", means explicitly that we are to share this peace, to work for it and, if necessary, suffer for it. It is meant for all people.

Messianic peace crowns the work of love and justice. It is a fruit of the Spirit that cannot be severed from the other gifts of the Spirit. Its messengers will therefore always act with kindness, benevolence, gentleness and patience; they will never lose heart and will be ever alert to the many opportunities to act as peacemakers and to radiate serenity.

The peace of Christ cannot be privatized. It surely takes hold of our inner being, but our heart's peace is building bridges to our neighbour; it is peace in all of life's relationships: in families, communities, neighbourhoods, in social, cultural, economic and political interactions. If all of us would celebrate the Memorial of the Lord as he intends it, there would be streams of peace flowing out to all the world, benefiting all humankind. We should never forget that Christ, who has reconciled us sinners, grants us his peace to do the same. It is his gift to us to be shared even with our enemies, those who calumniate us, insult us or hurt us in any way. They need to experience the peace of Christ through us.

Those who do the work of peace in Christ's name will be neither timid nor evasive. They will speak frankly and act with courage, never compromising the saving truth. But they will, in all their endeavours, try to reflect Christ, the Divine Word of Truth, who breathes love. If all our desires, words and actions arise from a grateful memory and a profound consciousness of our union with Christ, the Prince of Peace, then no inconvenience and no misunderstanding will affect our serenity and self-control. We shall be able to put into practice the words of St Paul: "If your enemy is hungry, feed him; if he is thirsty, give him a drink; by doing this you will heap live coals on his head. Do not let evil conquer you, but use good to defeat evil" (Rom 12:20-21).

Almighty God and Father,
we thank you for sending us Jesus Christ
as our Peace, our Reconciler.
We thank you that,
through Jesus Christ in the Eucharist,
you give us the kiss of peace.
We thank you for the mission to be peacemakers,
in which we can experience
that we are truly your children.
Send us your Holy Spirit,
so that ever-increasing gratitude
may motivate and guide us
in our mission of peace and justice.
Through Christ our Lord.
Amen.

16

Sharers in the divine nature

"Whoever eats my flesh and drinks my blood possesses eternal life, and I will raise him up on the last day. My flesh is real food; my blood is real drink. Whoever eats my flesh and drinks my bloods dwells continually in me and I dwell in him" (Jn 6:54-57).

"Happy are those who are called to his Supper!" With Communion, the Eucharist comes to its summit where our gratitude should be overflowing. What greater sign of his love could the Father give than to send us his Son to be our Saviour and our brother? And what greater sign could Jesus give than his body and blood to remind us that he lived, suffered, died and rose from the dead for us?

The theological reflection on Eucharistic communion touches the very heart of Christian prayer and life. These are to be seen in the light of the triune life of God, which is an ineffable dialogue and total sharing. The Father shares all that he is and has with his Word, in the Holy Spirit, who is the total mutual love and sharing. It is the central message, beautifully synthesized in the introduction to the First Letter of John, that we have become sharers of this divine life of communion. "Our theme is the word of life. This life was made visible; we have seen it and bear our testimony; we here declare to you the eternal life which dwelt with the Father and was made visible to us. What we have seen and heard we declare to you, so that you and we together may share a common life, that life which we share with the Father and his Son Jesus Christ" (1 Jn 1:2-3).

All of creation and the whole history of salvation are a mirror-image of the triune-sharing between the Father and the Son in the Holy Spirit. Through the grace of the Holy Spirit we are initiated into this life which, in the final beatitude, we will celebrate forever.

Especially the great Eucharistic discourse (Jn 6) and the farewell discourses and high-priestly prayer of Jesus (Jn 13-17) disclose to us this ineffable mystery. As the Father gives himself to his Word from his fullness, so creation and redemption are given to us, not because God needs them, but because they come from the fullness of sharing between the divine persons. As theology, within its human limits, has tried to explain it, their very personhood is a relationship of sharing. And we come to the full stature of personhood by gratefully receiving our share in this mystery. "Christ has bestowed on us everything that . . . enables us to know the One who called us by his own splendour and might. Through them he has given us his promises, great beyond all price, and through them you may come to share in the very being of God" (2 Pet 1:3-4).

Jesus, in his full humanity, has received as the gift of the Father a unique way of sharing, with the Divine Word. The hypostatic union between the divine and human nature of Jesus is the summit and source of God's sharing himself with his creatures. The Eternal Word of the Father is total Eucharist: abiding thanksgiving in the Holy Spirit who is the mutuality of gracious giving and receiving.

There is only one God; there is the one divine nature. But God's life is communion: blissful sharing. His works re-echo this divine dialogue-sharing. "When all things began, the Word already was. The Word dwelt with God, and what God was, the Word was. The Word, then, was with God at the beginning, and through him all things came to be; no single thing was created without him" (Jn 1:1-4).

Jesus' self-giving on the cross, where he entrusts himself to the Father while giving his life-blood for us, is the height of salvation history, the great event of the One who is anointed by the Spirit for this total sharing. He is the living Gospel in self-giving love. By making himself unreservedly our brother, indeed the servant of God and of humankind, the Son, to whom the Father has entrusted everything (Lk 10:22), shows that the Father loves us as he loves his Son.

In the Eucharistic communion, the Word Incarnate continues his divine and human thanksgiving by making us sharers of his life and, at the same time, sharers in his thanksgiving. Here he continues to proclaim: "I am the vine and you are the branches. He who dwells in me, as I dwell in him, bears much fruit; for apart from me you can do nothing" (Jn 15:5).

Making us participants in his glorious body and in the new and everlasting covenant, he manifests that he loves us with the very love with which the Father loves him (Jn 15:9). In the Eucharistic communion, the prayer of Christ, the prophetic high-priest, is perpetuated: "As thou, Father, art in me and I in thee, so also may they be in us" (Jn 17:21).

If all our life becomes thanksgiving to God and responsive appreciation of others, Christ gradually introduces us to the experience of being made sharers of the glory he has received from the Father. Humble and joyous gratitude removes the obstacles that could hinder us from being sharers of the divine nature; or rather, the Holy Spirit, the giver of life and of all good gifts, the gift between the Father and the Son, removes these obstacles if we do not resist. "When he comes, who is the Spirit of truth, he will guide you into all the truth; for he will not speak on his own authority but will tell only what he hears; and he will make known to you the things that are coming. He will glorify me, for everything that he makes known to you he will draw from what is mine. All that the Father has is mine, and that is why I said, 'Everything that he makes known to you he will draw from what is mine'" (Jn 16:13-15).

In this light we can best understand what the real presence of Christ in the Eucharistic communion means. Christ is not just "out there". As on the cross, so in the Eucharist, he comes to us in the power of the Holy Spirit in total self-bestowal. And by the same Spirit whom he sends to us, we can respond by giving our heart, mind, will and actions to him in the service of our brothers and sisters. Thus, and only thus, is the Eucharistic presence given full mutuality.

We receive the Holy Spirit according to the measure of our constant gratitude and generous readiness to put truth into practice. If we let ourselves be guided by the Holy Spirit in thankful response to Christ's self-bestowal, then our dialogue with our brethren will never end in empty words: in word and deed we give ourselves. Our life will be the overflow of our sharing in the divine nature. Thus, united with Christ, we live the morality of the Easter mystery. We no longer live selfishly for ourselves but for Christ, and we will love and serve each other for his sake. All this flows from the Eucharist and back to it, in a stream of grace and humble gratitude.

As the dialogue between the Father and the Son in the Holy Spirit is at the same time word and response, event and gift, overflowing in the work and word of creation and salvation, so our Eucharist and prayer-life will be nothing less than genuine self-bestowal: a response overflowing in faithful love for all the children of God and a commitment to justice and peace as a continuation of the Eucharistic sharing.

Thus, Christ, in and through us, will continue his response to the Father and his work of salvation for humankind, in the power of the Holy Spirit.

When, in our prayer and our daily life, we enter into these dimensions of the divine dialogue and sharing, our communion with the body and blood of Christ is a promise and pledge of eternal life. "Father, I desire that those who are thy gift to me may be with me where I am" (Jn 17:24).

Lord Jesus Christ,
we thank you for the praise and thanksgiving
you offer in your self-giving love to the Father
while calling us to share in your divine life
and in your mission
to make visible the love of the Father.
Send us your Holy Spirit,
so that, day by day,
we may better and more gratefully understand
the height and the depth, the length and the breadth
of the mystery of the Eucharistic communion.
Amen.

17

Eucharist: gift and mission

"They are strangers in the world, as I am. Consecrate them by the truth; thy word is truth. As thou hast sent me into the world, I have sent them into the world" (Jn 17:17-19).

After his final blessing, at the end of the Eucharistic celebration, the celebrant tells us that "the Mass is ended" and invites us to "go in peace". It is interesting to compare the new liturgy in the various languages. Most of them avoid anything like "The Mass is ended"; the emphasis now is *mission*. We are sent in the peace of Christ to do the work of peace.

If we have celebrated with heartfelt joy and gratitude, we shall understand that the kiss of peace, received from Christ and shared among the participants, issues in a life that continues to reflect this experience. When the risen Lord greets his disciples for the second time with "Peace be with you!", he immediately gives them their mission: "As the Father has sent me, so I send you" (Jn 20:21).

Reconciled, we shall work for reconciliation; graced we shall be gracious — ever more a true and efficacious image of the love of God, the peace of Christ, the rallying power of the Holy Spirit. The Eucharist — praise and thanksgiving — will always and everywhere be the leitmotif that gives direction and coherence to all our thoughts, desires, words and actions. We shall try to live this spirit of gratitude towards God and our neighbour and thus spread the peace of the Gospel.

When I was a seminarian, our professor of moral theology frequently used a book with the strange title, "Pastoral Chemistry", by Fattinger. Among many similar items, there were indications about how long it would take the Eucharistic species to be dissolved in view of the human body's chemical dispositions; and these chemical indications should instruct us about the length of our thanksgiving after Mass! A theological-spiritual vision has no place for any such reckoning. All our life should be lived in loving remembrance and active expression of gratitude.

Jesus has shared himself with us to increase our faith, hope, charity and vigilance in order to continue, in us and through us, his own mission to make the love of the Father visible to all people. He lives in us so that we can love each other with him and through him. We thus continue our Eucharistic thanksgiving. This means that we shall render thanks in good health and in bad health. We shall praise the Lord if we meet contradiction. We give thanks for a good sleep that restores our energies, but we will also use the sleepless hours to count our blessings from the Lord. We manifest gratitude and appreciation in our family, at work, in recreational activities, and through our commitment in the social, economic, cultural and political realms.

Christian spouses live the sacrament of matrimony in the perspective of the Eucharist by accepting each other as a gift of God, by mutual appreciation, kindness, patience and healing forgiveness. The Eucharistic person does not take refuge in escapism: "If only I had a husband/wife like my friend . . .". Those who gratefully love each other as they are can grow together in maturity and in a shared commitment to the kingdom of God and true progress on earth.

Christian parents who are moulded by the Eucharist

show appreciation, trust, gratitude towards their
children as they are: a gift of God and a mutual gift.
They accept the children with their limitations and thus
broaden the possibilities of growth in intelligence, skills,
and above all in the love of God and neighbour. And
since gratitude and appreciation become effective
encouragement, all will be more and more enabled
to discover their own inner resources and those of
others.

Living the Eucharist, we shall everywhere first discover and acknowledge the positive opportunities as
signs of God's presence and call. We will then be
better prepared to meet the challenges and hardships
of life in view of Christ's own redemptive suffering
in the battle against evil.

In the freedom we gain in this Eucharistic vision,
we shall believe in our vocation to holiness and will
bring into our life and the world around us the spirit
of the beatitudes. We shall not be caught in the slavery
of a utilitarian ideology nor manipulated by exploitive
manipulators. Rather, we shall use our talents and
charisms for the growth of genuine freedom in our
world.

Before each relevant decision, we shall ask ourselves:
can this or that desire, word, action be offered to the
Lord as a part of the sacrifice of praise and thanksgiving for all he has done for us? Are we, by acting
in a certain way, giving praise to the Father and the
Son in the Holy Spirit?

Almighty Father,
through your Son Jesus Christ you have revealed to us
how your will is done in heaven.
Through him and in him you have given us a share
in the communion between you and your Eternal Word
in the Holy Spirit.
As model of praise and thanksgiving,
you have sent us Jesus, our Master and brother.

Let your Holy Spirit come upon your Church
so that, in all her communities, she may be able
to celebrate the Eucharist with such faith and gratitude
that it becomes for all a peak-experience,
clear direction, light and strength for their life.
Send us priests
who are filled with the spirit of the Eucharist,
who can become an inspiration for many;
and laypeople who show us
how our life can be brought home into the Eucharist.
Through Christ our Lord.
Amen.